# Drug Abuse and Society™

# HEROIN
## The Deadly Addiction

ROSEN
PUBLISHING®
New York

Corona Brezina

Published in 2009 by The Rosen Publishing Group, Inc.
29 East 21st Street, New York, NY 10010

Copyright © 2009 by The Rosen Publishing Group, Inc.

First Edition

**Library of Congress Cataloging-in-Publication Data**

Brezina, Corona.
Heroin: the deadly addiction / Corona Brezina.—1st ed.
    p. cm.—(Drug abuse and society)
Includes bibliographical references.
ISBN-13: 978-1-4358-5017-0 (library binding)
1. Heroin. 2. Heroin abuse. 3. Heroin abuse—Treatment. I. Title.
HV5822.H4B74 2009
362.29'3—dc22

                                                    2008011788


*Manufactured in Malaysia*

# Contents

# INTRODUCTION

In one of the most vivid scenes from the movie *The Wizard of Oz*, Dorothy and her companions set out across a vivid field of poppies. Dorothy begins to stumble, her eyes closed, and she collapses into the flowers. The exact details aren't accurate—the scent of opium poppies do not cause any effects—but there's no doubt that Dorothy has fallen under the influence of opiates.

Poppy farmers would have viewed Dorothy's field as a potential source of illegal drug profit. The poppy sheds its petals shortly after blooming, and growers cut into the seed pod and harvest the sap. As it dries, the sap hardens into a dark brown gum—crude opium. Treatment with a few chemicals can isolate morphine, the active ingredient that gives opium its narcotic, or opioid, properties.

Farmers harvest opium from a field of poppies in the remote Jurum district of Afghanistan's northern Badakhshan province. Afghanistan's opium crop supplies most of the world's heroin.

Morphine, in turn, can be further refined by treatment and purification with more chemicals. The result is the drug diacetyl-morphine, known commonly as heroin. Most often, it is sold as a white or brownish powder. The chemical company Bayer thought that its new drug—the name of which is derived from the German *heroisch*, or "heroic"—had potential to treat tuberculosis when it was first marketed in 1898. The scientists who studied

5

the drug probably never suspected that in a hundred years, heroin would overshadow tuberculosis as a public health threat.

Heroin and morphine are opiates. Opiates are chemicals that are derived from opium. Codeine and oxycodone (sold as Percodan and the longer-lasting OxyContin) are also opiates.

Highly addictive and fatal at large doses, heroin was made illegal in 1956. Heroin is dangerous to the user; it can cause death, permanent health damage, and the deterioration of the quality of one's life. It is dangerous to others. Family and friends often feel the impact of the user's actions, and the user can unintentionally injure other people while impaired. It is dangerous to society. Heroin activity can tarnish communities, and one way or another, the public often ends up paying for a heroin addict's habit.

Despite these realities, about 1.5 percent of all Americans have tried heroin, according to the 2006 National Survey on Drug Use and Health (NSDUH). This equals about 3.8 million people. About 91,000 people had used the drug for the first time within the past year, and the average age of a first-time user was 20.7 years old. There was no major increase or decrease in these statistics for first-time users from 2005.

Rates of heroin use among prisoners is much higher, as reported by the Bureau of Justice. In 2004, about 23.5 percent of state prisoners and 17.9 percent of federal prisoners reported that they had tried heroin or other opiates. About 15 percent of state prisoners and 9.2 percent of federal prisoners indicated that they had used heroin regularly at some point in their lives, meaning at least once weekly for a month or longer.

The University of Michigan tracks the attitudes toward drugs of young people in their annual Monitoring the Future survey. In 2007, 1.3 percent of all eighth graders and 1.5 percent of all tenth and twelfth graders reported that they had tried heroin. When asked about their opinions on heroin use, 60.3 percent of eighth graders, 70.5 percent of tenth graders, and 60.2 percent of twelfth graders agreed that trying heroin once or twice without using a needle was a "great risk." When asked whether they thought it would be possible for them to obtain heroin, 12.6 percent of eighth graders, 17.3 percent of tenth graders, and 29.7 percent of twelfth graders responded that it would be "fairly easy" or "very easy" to obtain.

# CHAPTER 1
## A Brief History of Heroin

For about five thousand years, human beings have used opium for its properties as a painkiller. One of the earliest descriptions comes from the Greek physician Hippocrates (460 BCE), who wrote about the effects of "poppy juice." Opium was commonly used in Europe throughout the Middle Ages. During the early history of the United States, preparations containing opium were often prescribed as medications for virtually any ailment. Laudanum, a mixture containing alcohol, opium, and spices, gained wide popularity. Benjamin Franklin took medicines containing opium for his painful gout, a condition where uric acid crystals accumulate in joints, usually in the big toes.

Until the nineteenth century, opium abuse was not considered a social problem.

During the nineteenth century, opium was widely used to treat gastro-intestinal illness, respiratory conditions, and practically any other ailment. Opiate preparations were even given to teething infants.

Opium taken orally does not have an extremely potent effect, which lessened the likelihood of a severe addiction or deadly consequence. Gradually, though, the practice of smoking opium caught on. In 1804, a German pharmacist isolated morphine, the active ingredient in opium. In 1853, the hypodermic syringe was invented. Smoking and injection both delivered a stronger effect, and addiction rates began to climb. After the U.S. Civil War ended in 1865, morphine dependency became known as the "soldier's disease." Opium dens, where users would gather to smoke opium together, opened across the country.

In 1898, the German pharmaceutical company Bayer developed a new opium derivative to treat coughing caused by tuberculosis. It named its new medicine "heroin." For over a decade, heroin use was legal and considered safe.

As the abuse potential of heroin became obvious, laws were passed that gradually led to it being restricted and finally banned. Making heroin illegal did not end demand for the drug, however. Criminal organizations took over the production, trade, and distribution of heroin. Illegal laboratories were set up in Asia for heroin production. For many years, the Italian Mafia was one of the major crime syndicates involved in heroin sales. World War II, however, interrupted the global heroin trade. Supplies were low, and traffickers began the practice of "cutting" pure heroin with cheaper substances, reducing its purity.

Although parts of Asia are still major heroin producers today, most of the heroin distributed in the United States comes from Colombia and Mexico. The purity of the heroin has gradually risen even as the price of the drug has fallen.

Trends in heroin use have shifted throughout the decades. During the 1950s, heroin use was associated with the beat movement of writers and musicians who felt alienated from mainstream American culture. This included authors William S. Burroughs and Jack Kerouac and the jazz artist Miles Davis.

Using heroin in combination with other drugs—such as the mood-altering drug ecstasy—can increase the potentially lethal effects of both drugs.

A number of high-profile celebrities have struggled with heroin addiction, sometimes with tragic results.

Some drug users combine heroin with other illegal drugs, despite the greater risks of mixing two drugs. A speedball is a mixture of heroin and cocaine. As the drug ecstasy became popular in the 1990s, followed by an increase in methamphetamine

## Heroin's Soundtrack

There is a long-standing debate about drug references in music lyrics and their influence on teen substance abuse. Does a bombardment of drug references in popular music—as well as in books, movies, TV shows, and other sources of entertainment—increase the likelihood that teens will experiment with drugs?

There are valid points to both sides of the debate, but neither side denies the prevalence of drug references in pop culture. In a study released in 2008, researchers at the University of Pittsburgh School of Medicine tallied substance abuse references in the top songs of 2005. A third of the songs explicitly mentioned drugs, alcohol, or tobacco. According to their calculations, a teenager that listened to 2.4 hours of music every day would hear over thirty thousand substance abuse reference every year.

During their survey, the researchers probably listened to the 2005 song "She's Like Heroin" by the group System of a Down. Heroin has been a topic for a number of acclaimed songs over the years. The Velvet Underground featured two songs about heroin— "Heroin" and "I'm Waiting for the Man"—on a 1969 album. Songs about heroin do not always glamorize the drug. In his 1967 song "Cold Turkey," which never explicitly mentions heroin, John Lennon talks about the pain of withdrawal.

use, it became common for some users to combine these drugs with heroin.

## THE LURE OF HEROIN

In the past, most people have regarded heroin as the ultimate taboo "hard drug." Casual drug users, who were willing to experiment with marijuana or cocaine, would draw the line at trying heroin. Even some heroin users would draw yet another line at mainlining, or injecting, the drug directly into the bloodstream, especially after the onset of the AIDS epidemic, which was often spread through the use of shared needles.

However, during the 1990s, heroin began to attract new users: teenagers who did not share the older generation's aversion to heroin. Part of the reason for this was changing attitudes about drugs, both legal and illegal. Unlike previous generations, young people coming of age today take it for granted that practically any medical condition can be fixed with a prescription, whether it's depression, high cholesterol, or an injury. Acceptance of illegal drug use is a possible extension of this attitude.

The falling price and increasing purity of heroin also accounts for its increased popularity. In 1980, the average purity, or amount of heroin in the mixture, was less than 5 percent. At this low concentration, heroin must be injected in order to have an effect. Today, however, the average purity is over 35 percent, and depending on the batch, it might be much higher. Since the drug is

Heroin has become more readily available to young adults. Unlike in the past, a young user's dealer today may often be a fellow student.

so much stronger, it has a potent effect when smoked or snorted. To many teenagers, these methods of heroin use seem safer and easier than injection. Heroin became easier to obtain as well. Suburban high schoolers could buy it from friends or try it out at parties.

Heroin trends vary among different regions and demographic groups. In some parts of the West Coast of the United States, for example, rates of heroin addiction are particularly high due to the easy availability of a form of the drug called black tar heroin, which is imported from Mexico. Since it comes in a dark mass, this form must be dissolved and injected, increasing the risk of addiction as well as overdose.

# Myths and Facts

**Myth:** I don't have to worry about heroin overdose or addiction if I'm careful about the dosage.

**Fact:** The purity of heroin varies greatly, so it's not possible to know the heroin content of a single dose. Assuming that a dose is "safe" can be fatal, and the effects of the same amount of heroin may vary from one individual to another. Also, tolerance to heroin develops very quickly. Regardless of the dosage, most addicts don't realize that they have a drug problem until their drug use is out of control.

**Myth:** Heroin addicts can stop whenever they want if they just use their willpower.

**Fact:** Although some addicts can give up heroin on their own, most require help from professionals. Heroin users develop a powerful psychological and physical dependence on the drug. The phrase "quitting cold turkey" has its origins in how an addict's skin becomes cold and clammy due to withdrawal if he or she abruptly stops using the drug. Drug treatment programs can provide guidance and support for recovering addicts.

**Myth:** Since so many writers and artists have been linked to heroin, there must be some connection between heroin use and creative personalities.

**Fact:** In most cases, heroin abuse among celebrities best demonstrates how the drug can devastate their lives, not promote their art. Stories of famous heroin users describe tragedy and wasted potential. Although a few personalities managed to live with their addiction—William S. Burroughs died of natural causes at the age of eighty-three despite a lifetime of on-and-off heroin use—they are the rare exception.

# CHAPTER 2

## Abuse

After taking a dose of heroin, the user quickly feels the "rush" take hold of the body and brain. The drug often delivers an immediate sense of overpowering euphoria, which leads to a pleasant, dreamy state. Some people describe it as a kind of trance, while others say that it makes them feel like all of life's worries, anxieties, and stresses are suddenly gone.

The effects of heroin can vary greatly from one user to another. Despite heroin's reputation as one of the most alluringly pleasurable drugs, people can find it an unpleasant experience. For some, heroin may bring on disorientation and even hallucinations. Others find that the immediate unpleasant side effects of heroin, such as nausea, outweigh the enjoyable aspects.

# PHYSICAL AND PSYCHOLOGICAL EFFECTS

How does taking heroin trigger the "hit," or high, and other resulting effects? Once it enters the body, heroin is converted back into morphine. Upon reaching the brain, opiates affect the central nervous system, impacting both physical and psychological functioning.

Although heroin and morphine work the same way in the brain, heroin acts more quickly because of chemical modifications. When injected directly into a vein, it reaches the brain within ten seconds. Users may instead choose to inject into a muscle, called skin popping, rather than directly into the bloodstream. (This method is easier and less dangerous.) The effect produced by injecting into a muscle is more gradual, taking about five minutes to be felt.

Heroin can also be smoked, often through a method called "chasing the dragon," in which the drug

Intravenous heroin users often start out by injecting the drug into a vein in the arm. When the veins collapse, they move on to veins in other areas.

is placed on a piece of tin foil and heated from beneath. Users inhale the resulting vapor with a tube, and the effect is nearly as fast as with intravenous injection. The effect from snorting powdered heroin takes about ten to fifteen minutes to kick in.

The surge of euphoria, dulling of pain, and other sensations associated with heroin use is caused by the activity of certain nerve cells in the brain. Opiates work by binding to certain receptor molecules on nerve cells, receptors linked with stimulating pleasure and coping with pain. These receptors can also be activated by naturally occurring chemicals in the brain called endorphins and enkephalins, but activation occurs only to a limited extent. Opiates bombard the receptors. The resultant "rush" far exceeds any naturally occurring effect, activating what is known informally as one of the pleasure circuits in the brain.

Since opiates affect brain function, and the central nervous system controls all of the other systems of the body, heroin use causes a variety of physical side effects. It slows down breathing and motor skills, and it causes slurred speech. Users often go "on the nod" soon after taking a dose of the drug, slumping into a stupor and letting their eyelids droop. Some people find this a frightening experience, like a suffocating faint. If the state is broken, such as by a touch on the shoulder or an unexpected sound, it can provoke a startled or aggressive reaction.

The brain registers heroin as a toxin, triggering nausea, especially for first-time users, and sometimes vomiting. The pupils of the eyes contract, sometimes to pinpoints. Heroin can

A young addict hides out in a demolition house. Many heroin abusers neglect their health and well-being in their pursuit of the drug.

cause users to become flushed and sweaty. Opiates can trigger a release of histamine, which makes users' skin feel itchy. They also interfere with the digestive tract, causing constipation and other digestive problems.

The effects of heroin last between four and six hours. For someone who is not addicted, the dreamlike state slowly wears off. The user may have a hangover but not the symptoms of withdrawal. For addicts, however, "coming down" is much more difficult. Heroin changes the body chemistry of addicts, and as soon as the effects of one dose fade, addicts crave more.

Since heroin slows breathing, an overdose of the drug can quickly lead to respiratory failure, coma, and death. Symptoms of an overdose may include clammy skin, blue fingers and lips, and convulsions. Generally, an overdose can be reversed by an injection of the antidote drug naloxone if detected in time. It causes the opiates to be ejected from the receptor sites in the brain.

## RECOGNIZING SIGNS OF ABUSE

One day, a teenager is cheerful and communicative. The next day, she's moody and defensive. She's secretive, exhibits odd behavior, and sometimes has fits of temper for no good reason. These are some of the possible warning signs of a substance abuse problem, but—as any parent, teacher, or fellow student knows—they are often just a normal part of adolescent behavior.

For drug abusers, however, the drug habit begins to take a toll on their everyday lives. They lose interest in schoolwork and extracurricular activities. They may start hanging out with a new crowd of friends. They lie to hide their drug use and its consequences. Parents may be shocked to discover that their former model students are suddenly cutting class and stealing money from them. They may exhibit abnormal anxiety, depression, lethargy, aggressiveness, or other personality changes. Physical signs may include sudden weight loss, abnormal fatigue, or inattention to hygiene.

There's no single factor that drives teenagers to experiment with drugs. Some may turn to drugs as a way to deal with the pressures and anxieties of adolescence.

Heroin is one of the most potent and addictive illegal drugs. Most teens recognize that it is too dangerous to experiment with, but some adolescents believe that they're immune to the risks. Teenagers are constantly looking for new experiences and ideas. They might believe that trying heroin once, just to see what it's like, won't hurt. They may think that adults exaggerate the potential dangers. Sometimes, they're introduced to the drug by a friend or family member. In some cases, drug experimentation or other risky behaviors may be a symptom of underlying psychological problems.

Most new heroin users believe that they can control their use of the drug. They reason that if they use it only occasionally, they are in no danger of becoming addicted. Even after they become regular users, heroin abusers frequently remain in denial about the extent of their dependence on the drug.

Parents, friends, and teachers are often slow to recognize the warning signs of heroin abuse. They may have inaccurate preconceptions about the "typical" heroin user. Many people think that hard drugs are an inner-city problem, or that only the kids on the fringes of the social order at school would try heroin. In reality, heroin has spread to city suburbs and rural areas. The average age of users has fallen. Feature stories in newspapers may tell about the downfall of a star high school athlete or a promising young college graduate due to heroin. Old profiles of a "typical" heroin user are no longer accurate.

# Ten Great Questions to Ask a Drug Counselor

1. What resources are offered by my school or community for adolescents with substance abuse problems?
2. Some of my friends have told me that doing heroin once or twice is perfectly safe and that I should try it. What's the best way to let them know I'm not interested?
3. I think that one of my friends is using heroin, but he won't admit that he has a problem. Who can I talk to about getting help for him?
4. My friends think that my drug use is out of control, but I don't think I have a problem. How can I tell if I'm really addicted?
5. I'm too ashamed to admit to my parents that I have a drug problem. How can I approach them?
6. I'm recovering from a drug problem and I feel like I don't fit in at school anymore. How can I get back into my old routine?
7. I'm recovering from a drug problem and I'm constantly tempted to return to using heroin. How can I avoid relapsing?
8. I've used heroin in the past, and now I'm experiencing health problems. Could these have been caused by drug use?
9. A friend of mine is recovering from a heroin problem. How can I help support her?
10. I hurt a lot of people's feelings when I had a drug problem, and now they don't trust me. How can I repair our relationships?

# CHAPTER 3
## The Power of Addiction

Angela had a rocky relationship with her mother, so she spent as much time as she could out of the house with her friends. When she was seventeen, she started skipping school and experimenting with drugs. Her mother didn't realize anything was wrong until she got a call from Angela's school counselor. Angela was failing most of her classes.

Angela's mother confronted her, but she denied that she had a problem. A few weeks later, Angela's mother discovered that there was money and jewelry missing from her room. Again, she tried to talk to her daughter. Angela screamed at her and stormed out of the house. She didn't come back.

Angela moved in with some friends, and she dropped out of school. She had used heroin in the past, and now she developed a full-blown addiction. Heroin became the only thing she cared about. In the winter, an overdose sent her to the emergency room. There, she learned that she was eligible for a residential treatment program in her community. Desperate, Angela decided to try it.

At first, she felt sick and miserable. Staff members were constantly lecturing her and dictating how she had to spend every minute of her time. She initially felt too ashamed to talk about her experiences, but she slowly opened up to the other recovering teens in the program. Angela began thinking about the future again. Her advocate at the program helped her to find an apartment and a job, and she continued outpatient treatment while attending night classes. A year later, Angela was still free of heroin.

Many new heroin users think that they can manage their heroin use without becoming addicted to the drug. They will use it only every so often, maybe on weekends or at parties. They don't realize that a pattern of heroin use typically increases as the body develops a tolerance to heroin. This means that the user requires bigger doses of the drug to achieve the desired effect. Eventually, regular drug use becomes a more and more important part of the user's life. As the user starts taking heroin with increasing frequency, eventually he or she will begin to crave more of the drug as soon as a dose begins to wear off. Instead of being a source of pleasure, the drug becomes a necessity to stave off the pains of heroin withdrawal.

# The Pangs of Withdrawal

The human body quickly adapts to functioning with the constant presence of opiates, and when the effects of a dose of heroin wear off, the body must readjust to its absence. This is the reason for the physical signs of withdrawal. Many withdrawal symptoms are the opposite of heroin's initial effects on a first-time user. A new heroin user feels euphoria, warmth, and relief from pain, for example. Heroin use also causes constipation. A user going through withdrawal, by contrast, will experience restlessness and acute anxiety, chills, hypersensitivity to pain, and diarrhea.

The onset of withdrawal is marked by flulike symptoms such as a runny nose, sweating, and changes in body temperature. Further signs include muscle cramps and pains, irritability, and headaches. Withdrawal also often causes insomnia, which worsens addicts' ability to cope with the psychological effects of withdrawal. Symptoms peak in twenty-four to seventy-two hours and gradually subside over a period of about a week.

## WHAT IS ADDICTION?

Heroin users develop both a physical and psychological addiction to the drug. The body becomes accustomed to the presence of opiates. There is also some evidence that the brain adapts to having the "pleasure circuit" regularly stimulated. Many heroin users claim that they can never recapture what they experienced the first time they tried the drug. Recovering addicts often feel dysphoria, a general sense of unhappiness, which lasts for months after they quit heroin.

An addict is aware of the damage that drug use is inflicting on his life, but he cannot control his habit. It often takes a crisis or an intervention before an addict will seek help.

An addict is someone who compulsively uses heroin regardless of the consequences. Many heroin addicts inject heroin several times a day and show signs of withdrawal as a dose wears off. The craving for the drug and the obsession with obtaining more become the most important things in an addict's life.

Occasional heroin use does not automatically doom a user to addiction, but there's no sure way of gauging whether a person is

27

likely to become an addict. Studies have shown that there may be a genetic element to addiction, meaning that some tendency toward substance abuse could run in families. This does not mean that a child of a former addict will become an addict. It just suggests that if a person has a family history of substance abuse, he may be more vulnerable to addiction if he experiments with a highly addictive drug such as heroin. Beyond the family tree, there tend to be commonalities among the backgrounds of drug addicts. For example, drug abusers were more likely to hang out with peers who also used drugs. Drug addicts are more likely to report a history of physical or emotional abuse.

## THE CONSEQUENCES OF ADDICTION

Heroin is notorious for the devastation it wreaks on an addict's health and life. The drug itself, however, does not directly cause most of the long-term medical problems associated with heroin use. It is actually the risks and self-neglect associated with an addict's lifestyle that bring about long-term health damage.

For example, the practice of "backtracking," or withdrawing a small amount of blood into a syringe to ensure a good connection, contaminates the syringe with any diseases in the blood. Anybody else who uses the same syringe could be exposed to HIV, hepatitis, tuberculosis, or one of many other diseases.

"Cooking" heroin is generally not a sterile process either, and contaminants from the drug or the paraphernalia can irritate

An overdose of intravenously injected heroin suppresses breathing. A user can slip into a coma within a matter of minutes.

veins. If a drug user takes the drug with a piece of cotton cloth, he or she may inadvertently inject tiny fragments of cotton along with the drug, causing the flulike "cotton fever" from an immune reaction. Repeated injection in the same veins often leads to irritation, called phlebitis, and the user then must inject other sites. Fragments of undissolved heroin and other contaminants can cause permanent damage to blood vessels and other parts of the body.

Although mainlining is the most dangerous method of use, anybody who tries heroin will be exposed to additives used to "cut" heroin, or dilute its purity. There's no way of knowing the exact composition of a dose of heroin—it might contain sugar, talcum powder, quinine, other drugs such as caffeine or amphetamine, or even poisonous substances such as strychnine. The additives used to cut heroin can be toxic or, in some people, provoke an allergic reaction. They may cause respiratory illness if snorted.

As the heroin habit takes over an addict's life, he or she may begin to neglect hygiene, nutrition, and exercise. Addicts may lose weight, develop a weakened immune system, and take dangerous risks in order to satisfy their drug habit. Their desperation and impaired judgment can lead to disastrous results. Heroin addicts can alienate their friends and relatives, lose their jobs and homes, and face the legal repercussions of their actions. The broader consequences of heroin use affect families, communities, the legal system, and society in general.

# CHAPTER 4

# The Law

In 1914, the passage of the Harrison Narcotic Act by Congress became the first measure intended to regulate drug use in the United States. The new law placed stiffer regulations on derivatives of coca (the source of cocaine) and opium. Both drugs were still legal, but now there were new taxes and restrictions that applied to their sale. Overall, the Harrison Act failed to curb drug use. Instead, it caused many morphine and codeine addicts to switch to heroin, which was cheaper and more potent, and it drove addicts to the black market.

During the 1920s, domestic heroin production was made illegal and new international controls reduced the global supply of opium. Heroin was not completely outlawed until 1956, when the Narcotic

Control Act stiffened penalties for drug offenses. In 1970, the Comprehensive Drug Abuse Prevention and Control Act overhauled and consolidated all previous drug laws. The principles behind this law are still in place today.

In 1972, President Richard Nixon declared a war on drugs, and he oversaw the creation of the Drug Enforcement Administration (DEA) in 1973. In 1982, as abuse of crack cocaine began to spread in the United States, President Ronald Reagan announced yet another war on drugs. The Federal

A woman tends to her poppy fields in Colombia. Officials attempt to curb poppy and coca cultivation through antidrug operations and by offering incentives to switch to legal crops.

Bureau of Investigation (FBI) was also given authority over drug activity in 1982. Although Reagan's war on drugs concentrated on reducing supply by fighting the international drug trade, new laws passed during the 1980s dramatically increased the number of offenders imprisoned for drug possession.

In the early 1990s, Colombia—a longtime supplier of cocaine—began producing heroin as well. Today, most of the heroin that is smuggled into the United States comes from Colombia, which tends to supply the East Coast, and Mexico, which supplies the West Coast. Antidrug trafficking efforts in Colombia tend to be complicated by internal politics in the country.

## Opium Production in Afghanistan

Although most of the heroin smuggled into the United States comes from countries to the south, the drug-producing nation that causes the American government the most concern is an ocean away. Afghanistan is the world's top grower of opium poppies, producing over 90 percent of all opiates. In 2006, there was a record-breaking crop of opium poppies, and the yield in 2007 was 34 percent higher. More cropland in Afghanistan is devoted to growing poppies and other drug crops than in Colombia, Peru, and Bolivia (all major coca growers) combined.

For the United States, the opium situation in Afghanistan goes beyond the issue of drug production. A coalition led by the United States invaded Afghanistan in 2001 in order to combat terrorism and install a democratic government. The thriving opium industry represents a failure on the part of the Americans to bring stability and economic security to Afghanistan.

## THE LAW

The Comprehensive Drug Abuse Prevention and Control Act of 1970 categorized drugs by five "schedules," according to their potential for abuse. Schedule I drugs are the most tightly controlled, with a high potential for abuse and no accepted medical use. Schedule V drugs, which are not tightly controlled, have legitimate medical uses and do not require a prescription from a doctor. Heroin and many other potent opiates and opioids are classified as Schedule I controlled substances.

So what is the penalty for possessing heroin? It must be understood that "possession" of a drug in a legal sense means having the drug in your control, not necessarily on your body or with your belongings. If the drug is in a room that you share with others, for example, the police may conclude that you are in possession.

Laws concerning illegal drugs are difficult to navigate. They vary depending on whether federal or state jurisdiction applies, and they vary from one state to the next. Drug laws are amended frequently. Federal and some state laws have guidelines for sentencing offenders, while others allow the prosecutor, judge, and other officials involved in the case to consider extenuating factors.

Depending on the offense, a drug crime can be considered a misdemeanor or a felony. A misdemeanor is a minor crime punishable by community service or a short jail sentence. A felony is a serious crime punishable by a harsh sentence. Possession of between one hundred grams and one kilo (about 3.5 to 35 ounces) of heroin carries a federal sentence of at least five years in prison. Possession of more than one kilogram carries a minimum ten-year sentence.

Certain factors are likely to increase penalties. Individuals can be prosecuted for "conspiracy" with a drug offender even if they did not commit a crime—for instance, letting the drug offender borrow a car could be interpreted as aiding a drug offense. Prosecutors may push for an "intent to distribute" conviction—punishable by a tougher sentence than possession—even if the offender claims a drug stash was for his or her own use. Adults get particularly stiff sentences for committing a drug offense within a school zone and for supplying minors with drugs. Repeat offenders receive harsher sentences than first-time offenders.

Communities sometimes designate schools, parks, and other places children congregate as drug-free zones. They generally extend 1,000 feet (305 meters) around the area.

# THE DRUG POLICY DEBATE

Is the United States winning the war on drugs? Supporters of current antidrug policies point out that sting operations by the DEA have disrupted Mexican and Colombian drug cartels and intercepted tons of heroin destined for the United States. They believe that strict sentencing for drug offenders is justified and that it acts as a deterrent for would-be drug users.

Reform advocates counter that efforts to curb drug trafficking have not reduced the flow of heroin into the United States. They claim that strict sentencing has packed prisons with nonviolent minor drug offenders at taxpayer expense.

It is unlikely that there will be any significant trend toward loosening the drug laws in the near future. No lawmaker wants to be viewed as "soft on drugs," unwilling to punish offenders. When President Bill Clinton took office in 1993, it was predicted that he would have a more lenient stance on drugs than the presidents before him. Instead, Clinton poured money into antidrug programs during his presidency, and he appointed retired four-star military general Barry McCaffrey to serve as "drug czar" and coordinate antidrug efforts. Nevertheless, the number of heroin users doubled between 1993 and 2000.

Drug policy is a hotly debated issue. Strong enforcement of drug laws and high incarceration rates are very expensive. Would money be better spent on increasing drug education, prevention efforts, and rehabilitation of addicts? Marijuana has been shown to

U.S. general Barry McCaffrey tours the Tres Esquinas military base in Colombia during a trip intended to promote antidrug efforts.

have some medical benefits. Should the government decriminalize medical marijuana use, or would this send a message condoning the use of illicit substances in general?

There is virtually no chance that heroin will ever be widely legalized, but it does have potential medical uses. As a painkiller, heroin has one major advantage over morphine: it reaches the brain more quickly. Some doctors believe that administration of heroin could help alleviate the pain of terminal (dying) cancer patients.

# CHAPTER 5

## Addiction Recovery

A heroin addict's life can quickly crumble. The consequences of the habit can cost him his job and the support of family and friends. Feeding the habit can leave him destitute. A squalid lifestyle can wreck his health. He lives with the constant danger of a heroin overdose. Eventually, he may have to pay the legal consequences for drug offenses.

The heroin addict may feel that he is alone in the world except for his addiction, but his actions affect the people around him, his community, and society. His family and friends are devastated and may devote time and money to try to help him. His employer feels his absence. When he buys heroin, the money may go to gangs or other criminal organizations that bring pain and violence to his city or region. Taxpayers may foot the bill for his medical care. If he goes to trial for a drug offense, taxpayers may also have to pay for both the prosecution and defense, if he is represented by a public defender. If he is convicted, taxpayers would pay for his rehabilitation or, as is far more likely, his incarceration. A year of drug treatment costs about $4,000. Keeping a convict in prison for a year, on the other hand, costs over $20,000.

## CALLING IT QUITS

This scenario does not have to end with prison and a ruined life, though. Giving up heroin is difficult and painful, but it's possible for addicts to end their dependence on the drug and turn their lives around.

Some heroin addicts recognize their drug problem before it can take a toll on their lives. Others refuse to admit to their addiction until they hit bottom, triggered by an event such as expulsion from school, an overdose, or an accident. Some users require an intervention, in which family or friends formally express their concern and urge the user to get help.

Heroin addiction is very difficult to break. For this reason, the best course for recovering addicts is to enter a drug treatment program run by experienced professionals. Drug abusers enrolled in outpatient programs attend group counseling and therapy

A group of teenagers participate in a drug rehabilitation session. Peer support and group interactions can be invaluable in helping teens recover from addiction.

daily or a few times a week, depending on the intensity of the program. This is a good option for many adolescents, since they can still live at home and attend school.

Teens with more severe drug abuse problems may require residential treatment programs. This often consists of a three- to six-week stay at a hospital or other treatment center followed up by outpatient treatment. Activities are tightly scheduled and include a combination of group sessions, exercise, study time, and everyday activities such as meals. These programs often stress a sense of solidarity among residents. There are also long-term residential programs called therapeutic communities intended for adolescent addicts.

Normally, a heroin addict begins to go through withdrawal within hours to a few days after his or her last dose. Withdrawal is unpleasant, but it is not life threatening.

There are two primary approaches to treating heroin addiction. One method is to replace heroin with another opiate that is less potent and dangerous. The most common substitute is the opioid methadone, which shares some common effects with heroin. Methadone staves off withdrawal and the craving for heroin but does not itself give the "high" of heroin. It also blocks the euphoric properties of heroin, so the two drugs cannot be used in combination. An addict may stay on methadone indefinitely— called methadone maintenance—or may wean him- or herself off by taking gradually smaller doses. A newer heroin substitute is buprenorphine, an opioid that needs to be taken only every few days and produces milder withdrawal symptoms than methadone.

The other method of treatment is detoxification, in which addicts go through supervised withdrawal without a maintenance drug. Patients are instead treated for the symptoms of withdrawal. They may take a drug called clonidine to lessen feelings of anxiety, as well as painkillers, sleeping aids, and anticonvulsants, but these

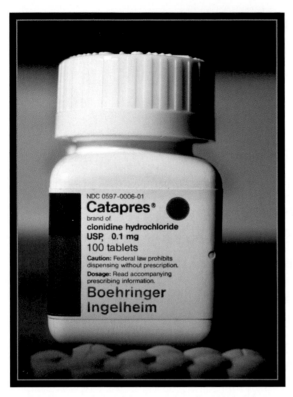

Addicts quitting heroin often take the prescription drug clonidine (Catapres) to reduce withdrawal pains. It relieves some of the flulike symptoms and lessens restlessness and anxiety.

medications do not completely eliminate the discomfort of the withdrawal period.

The path to recovery from drug addiction is not easy, and the relapse rate for former heroin addicts is very high. Upon returning to school, a teenager might start hanging out with the same crowd again and may return to using drugs as well. A former addict may be unable to cope with depression, anxiety, and other psychological troubles that might linger long after physical withdrawal has passed. The teen might think that using the drug just one time, perhaps at a party, won't bring about a return to addiction.

Recovering users often have trouble staying away from heroin unless they completely change their lifestyle. Addicts tend to react to certain triggers related to drug use—smokers might habitually light a cigarette after a meal or reach for one during a stressful situation. In the same way, the sight of drug paraphernalia or a visit from a former drug buddy might cause cravings for heroin. A recovering addict has a better chance of avoiding relapse if he can avoid reminders of heroin use.

It doesn't help that the transition back into normal life can be difficult. As they work their way through drug treatment programs, addicts are often forced to address the issues that drove them to try drugs in the first place. In addition, they will have to face new problems caused by their addictions. They may have to

## Drug Testing for Opiates

Many companies, as well as the federal government, require that their employees submit to drug testing at the workplace. The reasons are obvious. Drug use can undermine an employee's reliability, productivity, and overall health. In some occupations, an employee impaired by drug use can be a public safety hazard. Some employers refuse to hire people who have any sort of criminal drug record.

Hair, blood, sweat, and saliva can all be tested to determine drug use, but urine testing is the most common means. Traces of opiates remain in urine for up to four days following use, and an indicator unique to heroin remains detectable for two to eight hours after use. Opioids such as methadone do not yield a positive test, although eating about a teaspoon of poppy seeds will indeed result in a positive test for opiates.

43

fix relationships, resolve legal situations, deal with financial issues, and regain their health.

## REDUCING THE RAVAGES OF ABUSE

Methadone substitution and other treatment programs can enable former heroin addicts to make something of their lives, but some critics claim that methadone treatment merely exchanges one addiction for another. Even proponents have mixed feelings.

Protesters in Middlesboro, Kentucky, rally to express their opposition to a methadone clinic in their mountain region.

Drug treatment organizations often receive complaints from neighbors when they propose opening a new methadone clinic. Residents may say that although they respect the work the organization is doing, they don't want drug addicts hanging around near their homes.

Some other programs intended to help drug addicts are even more controversial. These "harm-reduction" programs focus on reducing the likelihood of overdose and other risks associated with heroin use. One tactic is offering syringe and needle exchanges, in which an addict can confidentially trade used syringes and needles for sterile ones. Needle-exchange programs have been shown to reduce the transmission of HIV and other diseases among drug users. Harm-reduction programs also educate participants on minimizing risk when using heroin and may teach how to recognize and respond to an overdose. Some states and communities operate harm-reduction programs, although the federal government does not. Opponents of harm-reduction programs allege that such measures condone drug use and that addicts should instead be punished for illegal drug activity.

# CHAPTER 6
## Heroin and the Media

The media have never had an easy job of covering drug issues. Conservatives accuse the "liberal media" of not casting drug use in enough of a negative light. Liberals accuse the media of parroting national drug policy without in-depth analysis. The media have the job of objectively reporting stories on drugs that could be easily sensationalized, politically charged, or offensive to some citizens.

Media coverage of drug stories often intersects with drug references in popular culture. Quentin Tarantino's violent movie *Pulp Fiction* was accused of glamorizing and misrepresenting heroin use. (The movie features an overdose victim being revived by a dose of adrenaline injected directly into the heart. Though a dramatic on-screen rescue, it's not a treatment for overdose.)

The British film *Trainspotting* earned highly favorable reviews with critics but ignited controversy due to its graphic depiction of heroin addiction among a group of friends.

The movie *Trainspotting*, which followed the story of several heroin addicts in Scotland, sparked an intense debate over whether the movie glamorized addiction.

## EARLY SENSATIONALISM

From the beginning, the media did not hesitate to play up the dangers of heroin. In the late 1890s and early years of the

47

twentieth century, there was a national hysteria over opium dens run by Chinese immigrants. Although many Americans were addicted to non-prescription medicines containing morphine and heroin, opium addiction was branded a "Chinese vice" threatening to subvert society.

One of the early opponents of heroin, Richmond Pearson Hobson, exploited the media's tendency toward sensationalism, publicizing his views in lectures laced with questionable facts and statistics. He started out as an advocate of prohibition, the banning of alcohol. "Ninety-five percent of all acts and crimes of violence are committed by drunkards," he declared, as quoted in Julian Durlacher's *Heroin*. Prohibition failed, and by 1928, he had changed his focus: "Most of the daylight robberies, daring hold-ups, cruel murders, and similar crimes of violence are now known to be committed chiefly by drug addicts." Hobson helped convince Americans that heroin use was causing a national crisis.

Hobson also argued that "drug addiction is more communicable [easily spread] and less curable than leprosy." This view still held sway in 1956, when heroin was made illegal by the passage of the Narcotic Control Act. Senator Price Daniel was one of the first supporters of the act. During the hearings, he repeated Hobson's quote about heroin and suggested that for incurable addicts, "it is just as humane to put them in some kind of colony."

## Heroin Chic

During the 1990s, the heroin chic trend briefly became popular in the fashion world. Stick-thin models in magazine spreads stared out dully at the reader with hollow, dark-rimmed eyes. A notorious ad campaign for a Calvin Klein fragrance featured emaciated models contorted into bizarre positions. The heroin chic look was widely criticized. The main concern with the popularization of heroin chic was how the trend glamorized the physical effects of heroin abuse.

Initially, the problem was with the models' appearance, not with actual alleged heroin use by models. It gradually became known, however, that a number of models had crossed over to heroin use. In 1997, twenty-year-old photographer Davide Sorrenti, one of the pioneers of the heroin chic look, was found dead of a heroin overdose. Public outcry and censure within the fashion industry ended the popularity of the heroin chic trend.

# CELEBRITIES IN THE SPOTLIGHT

Heroin thus established its reputation as the ultimate hard drug early on. Other drugs have since been closely watched. The use of hallucinogens such as LSD by young adults sparked anxiety during the 1960s and 1970s. The crack epidemic of the 1980s was seen as one of the most devastating symptoms of inner cities in crisis. The meth epidemic of the early twenty-first century has raised concern about the prevalence of the drug methamphetamine in rural and suburban America.

Law enforcement officers clean up a suspected methamphetamine lab in rural Niota, Tennessee. Although it was developed in 1919, methamphetamine has seen a recent surge in popularity.

Although the media have always reported on heroin abuse, availability, and other related points, they have never declared a specific "heroin epidemic" in which it became a social issue. That is not to say that the media have ignored teen heroin use. Many newspapers and other media periodically profile ordinary teens whose lives become derailed by heroin. The annual Monitoring the Future survey examines teens' use and perception of heroin, as well as other drugs. There are regions in which teen heroin use is unusually high, and occasionally a particular school or community will experience a heroin craze.

Coverage of heroin in the media, however, has centered on heroin abuse by celebrities, especially when it contributed to their downfall. During the early years of bebop and jazz, many musicians were linked to heroin. Saxophonist Charlie Parker and singer Billie Holiday both struggled with heroin addiction. As rock 'n' roll came into fashion, heroin use became associated with the lifestyle of some rockers. Jim Morrison of the Doors, Janis Joplin, singer Nico of the Velvet Underground, Keith Richards of the Rolling Stones, punk rocker Sid Vicious of the Sex Pistols, and many others allegedly struggled with heroin abuse. During the 1990s, the association between heroin and rock music went through another cycle. Many rockers of the grunge movement popularized in Seattle were linked to heroin. Most tragic was the case of Kurt Cobain of Nirvana, who struggled with heroin addiction before committing suicide.

On June 6, 2006, seventeen-year-old Joseph Krecker was found slumped over in his Jeep Cherokee in Chicago's West Side. The cause of his death was easily determined: Krecker was still clutching a bag of heroin.

Joseph Krecker should have had a bright future in front of him. He was a good athlete and well-liked at school. He had graduated from high school in the spring. But Krecker had a troubled side. He had started using heroin back in January, and in April, he confessed his addiction to his father, a suburban deputy police chief. Krecker checked into rehab.

Krecker's death occurred among a string of heroin-related fatalities and non-lethal overdoses. The cause of the outbreak was a concoction of potent heroin mixed with a prescription opioid drug called fentanyl. Used as a pain-relief medication or an anesthetic, fentanyl is about eighty times more powerful than morphine. Combined with heroin, it greatly increases the potential for overdose.

The drug combination quickly earned the nickname "Get High or Die Trying." Authorities warned the public about the dangers of the mixture, but the strategy backfired. Addicts swarmed the areas where they thought they might obtain the fentanyl-laced heroin, and the death count continued to rise. Between May and July, there were more than four hundred deaths attributed to the mixture across the Midwest and the East Coast.

More than a century after heroin was first made, it is still destroying lives and causing heartbreak. It has survived numerous

Recently, authorities discovered a 2,400-foot-long (732-meter-long) tunnel on the U.S.-Mexico border used to smuggle drugs into the United States. It was equipped with electric lights and ventilation.

attempts to stem its availability and abuse. As the outbreak of heroin–fentanyl deaths demonstrates, drug trends evolve over time. (The source of the mixture is believed to have been a laboratory in Mexico, which was later raided by the Mexican police.) There are many resources that alleviate some aspects of the heroin problem—education, prevention, harm–reduction programs, drug treatment, interdiction, incarceration—but after a century of debate, the only point of agreement on all sides of the issue is that with heroin, there's no easy solution.

# GLOSSARY

**addiction** The state in which a user is physically or psychologically dependent on a drug and feels compelled to keep taking it.

**anesthetic** A substance that causes loss of sensation or loss of consciousness.

**cartel** A consortium of organizations formed to regulate production, prices, and distribution of a good or service.

**dysphoria** An emotional state characterized by feelings of anxiety, depression, and discontent.

**euphoria** An emotional state characterized by feelings of elation or well-being.

**felony** A serious crime; specifically, a federal crime for which the punishment may be death or imprisonment for more than a year.

**intravenous** Injected directly into a vein.

**misdemeanor** A minor crime; specifically, one punishable by a fine and by a term of imprisonment less than one year.

**morphine** A crystalline alkaloid drug derived from opium.

**narcotic**  A drug that induces numbness or stupor.

**opiate**  A drug that contains opium or an opium derivative.

**opioid**  A synthetic compound that possesses some properties characteristic of opiates.

**paraphernalia**  Relating to drug use, implements used for preparing or taking drugs.

**sterile**  Free of living bacteria and other microorganisms.

**strychnine**  A highly poisonous compound used to kill rodents; it was formerly used in medicine as a stimulant.

**tolerance**  A characteristic of certain drugs in which the effects diminish with continued use, so that the user has to take larger doses to achieve the desired effects.

**trafficker**  One who engages in illegal or improper commercial activity.

**tuberculosis**  An infectious disease of humans and animals that especially affects the lungs.

**withdrawal**  Symptoms that occur when a habitual drug user suddenly stops taking a drug.

# FOR MORE INFORMATION

Center for Substance Abuse Prevention (CSAP)
Rm. 12-105 Parklawn Building
5600 Fishers Lane
Rockville, MD 20857
(301) 443-8956
Web site: http://www.samhsa.gov/centers/csap/csap.html
CSAP works with states and communities to develop comprehensive
prevention systems that create healthy communities in which people enjoy
a quality life. This includes supportive work and school environments,
drug- and crime-free neighborhoods, and positive connections with
friends and family.


Drug Enforcement Administration (DEA)
2401 Jefferson Davis Highway
Alexandria, VA 22301
(202) 307-1000
Web site: http://www.usdoj.gov/dea

The DEA is the Department of Justice organization charged with enforcing drug laws and developing antidrug programs all across the United States.

Narcotics Anonymous
P.O. Box 9999
Van Nuys, CA 91409
(818) 773-9999
Web site: http://www.na.org
Narcotics Anonymous is an international, community-based association of recovering drug addicts in over 127 countries worldwide.

National Institute on Drug Abuse
Neuroscience Center Building
6001 Executive Boulevard
Rockville, MD 20852
(301) 443-1124
Web site: http://www.nida.nih.gov
This is one of the leading organizations supporting research on drug abuse and addiction.

Office of National Drug Control Policy
P.O. Box 6000
Rockville, MD 20849-6000
(800) 666-3332

Web site: http://www.whitehousedrugpolicy.gov
This is the office charged with establishing policies, priorities, and objectives for the drug control program of the United States.

## WEB SITES

Due to the changing nature of Internet links, Rosen Publishing has developed an online list of Web sites related to the subject of this book. This site is updated regularly. Please use this link to access the list:

http://www.rosenlinks.com/daas/hero

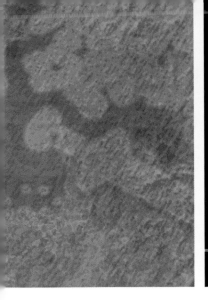

# FOR FURTHER READING

Bayer, Linda. *Drugs, Crime, and Criminal Justice*. Philadelphia, PA: Chelsea House, 2001.

Burgess, Melvin. *Smack*. New York, NY: HarperTeen, 2003.

Egendorf, Laura K. *Chemical Dependency: Opposing Viewpoints*. Farmington Hills, MI: Greenhaven Press, 2003.

Howard, Todd. *Heroin*. Farmington Hills, MI: Lucent Books, 2002.

Hyde, Margaret O., and John F. Setaro. *Drugs 101: An Overview for Teens*. Brookfield, CT: Twenty-First Century Books, 2003.

Rodriguez, Joseph. *Juvenile*. New York, NY: PowerHouse Books, 2004.

Roleff, Tamara, ed. *The War on Drugs: Opposing Viewpoints*. Farmington Hills, MI: Greenhaven Press, 2004.

Youngs, Bettie B., Jennifer Leigh Youngs, and Tina Moreno. *A Teen's Guide to Living Drug-Free*. Deerfield Beach, FL: Health Communications, Inc., 2003.

# BIBLIOGRAPHY

Babbit, Nikki. *Adolescent Drug and Alcohol Abuse: How to Spot It, Stop It, and Get Help for Your Family*. Sebastopol, CA: O'Reilly & Associates, 2000.

Bone, James. "First Murder Charge Over Heroin Mix That Killed 400." *Times* (London), August 26, 2006. Retrieved February 1, 2008 (http://www.timesonline.co.uk/tol/news/world/us_and_americas/article619947.ece).

Dunham, Will. "Study Finds Popular Music Awash in Booze, Drugs." Reuters, February 5, 2008. Retrieved February 8, 2008 (http://www.reuters.com/article/healthNews/idUSN0144737220080205).

Durlacher, Julian. *Heroin: Its History and Lore*. London, England: Carlton Books, 2000.

Emmett, David, and Graeme Nice. *Understanding Street Drugs: A Handbook of Substance Misuse for Parents, Teachers and Other Professionals*. 2nd ed. Philadelphia, PA: Jessica Kingsley Publishers, 2006.

Fabricant, M. Chris. *Busted! Drug War Survival Skills from the Buy to the Bust to Begging for Mercy*. New York, NY: HarperCollins, 2005.

Fuoco, Michael A. "Deaths, Overdoses Ebbing from Fentanyl-Laced Heroin." *Pittsburgh Post-Gazette*, August 14, 2006. Retrieved February 1, 2008 (http://www.post-gazette.com/pg/06226/713361-85.stm).

Gahlinger, Paul. *Illegal Drugs: A Complete Guide to Their History, Chemistry, Use, and Abuse*. New York, NY: Plume, 2004.

Ketcham, Katherine, and Nicholas A. Pace, M.D. *Teens Under the Influence: The Truth About Kids, Alcohol, and Other Drugs—How to Recognize the Problem and What to Do About It*. New York, NY: Ballantine Books, 2003.

Kuhn, Cynthia, et al. *Buzzed: The Straight Facts About the Most Used and Abused Drugs from Alcohol to Ecstasy*. 2nd ed. New York, NY: W. W. Norton and Company, 2003.

Kuhn, Cynthia, et al. *Just Say Know: Talking with Kids About Drugs and Alcohol*. New York, NY: W. W. Norton and Company, 2002.

Office of National Drug Control Policy. "Drug Facts: Heroin." January 24, 2008. Retrieved February 1, 2008 (http://www.whitehousedrugpolicy.gov/drugfact/heroin).

Sonder, Ben. *All About Heroin*. New York, NY: Franklin Watts, 2002.

Weil, Andrew, M.D., and Winifred Rosen. *From Chocolate to Morphine: Everything You Need to Know About Mind-Altering Drugs*. New York, NY: Houghton Mifflin Company, 1998.

Wintour, Patrick. "Opium Economy Will Take 20 Years and
£1bn to Remove." *Guardian* (London), February 6, 2008.
Retrieved February 8, 2008 (http://www.guardian.co.uk/
world/2008/feb/06/afghanistan.politics).

WMAQ-TV Chicago. "Chief Makes Landmark Arrest in Son's
Fatal OD Case." NBC5.com, August 24, 2006. Retrieved
February 1, 2008 (http://www.nbc5.com/targetchicago/
9733395/detail.html).

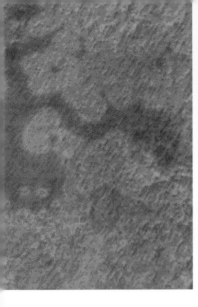

# INDEX

## ABOUT THE AUTHOR

Corona Brezina has written more than a dozen titles for Rosen Publishing. Several of her previous books have also focused on topics related to current events and issues facing young adults, including *Work Readiness: Great Decision-Making Skills* and *Violence and Society: Deadly School and Campus Violence*. She lives in Chicago.

## PHOTO CREDITS

P. 5 AFP/Getty Images; p. 9 © Collection of the New York Historical Society/Bridgeman Art Library; p. 11 David Hallett/Getty Images; p. 14 © www.istockphoto.com/Matty Symons; p. 17 © Itani/Alamy; p. 19 © Harald Theissen/imagebroker/Alamy; p. 21 Christina Kennedy/DK Stock/ Getty Images; p. 27 © www.istockphoto.com/Jennifer Fair; p. 29 © Simon Belcher/Alamy; p. 32 Rodrigo Arangua/AFP/Getty Images; p. 35 © pttmedical/Newscom; p. 37 Piero Pomponi/Getty Images; p. 40 Barros & Barros/The Image Bank/Getty Images; p. 42 © Custom Medical Stock Photo; pp. 44, 50 © AP Images; p. 47 © Miramax/Everett Collection; p. 53 Sandy Huffaker/Getty Images.

Designer: Tahara Anderson; Editor: Nicholas Croce
Photo Researcher: Amy Feinberg